W9-CEW-434

BROWN

By AMANDA DOERING
Illustrations by KELLAN STOVER
Music by ERIK KOSKINEN

CANTATA
LEARNING

WWW.CANTATALEARNING.COM

CANTATA
LEARNING

Published by Cantata Learning
1710 Roe Crest Drive
North Mankato, MN 56003
www.cantatalearning.com

Library of Congress Cataloging-in-Publication Data
Names: Doering, Amanda F., 1980– author. | Stover, Kellan, illustrator. |
   Koskinen, Erik, composer.
Title: Brown / by Amanda Doering ; illustrated by Kellan Stover ; music by
   Erik Koskinen.
Description: North Mankato, MN : Cantata Learning, [2018] | Series: Sing your
   colors! | Audience: Ages 4–7. | Audience: K to grade 3. | Includes lyrics
   and sheet music. | Includes bibliographical references.
Identifiers: LCCN 2017017534 (print) | LCCN 2017038293 (ebook) | ISBN
   9781684101504 (ebook) | ISBN 9781684101399 (hardcover : alk. paper) | ISBN
   9781684101962 (pbk. : alk. paper)
Subjects: LCSH: Brown--Juvenile literature. | Colors--Juvenile literature. |
   Children's songs, English.
Classification: LCC QC495.5 (ebook) | LCC QC495.5 .D62825 2018 (print) | DDC
   535.6--dc23
LC record available at https://lccn.loc.gov/2017017534

Book design and art direction, Tim Palin Creative
Editorial direction, Kellie M. Hultgren
Music direction, Elizabeth Draper
Music arranged and produced by Erik Koskinen

Printed in the United States of America in North Mankato, Minnesota.
122017   0378CGS18

ACCESS THE MUSIC!

SCAN
CODE
WITH
MOBILE
APP

CANTATALEARNING.COM

TIPS TO SUPPORT LITERACY AT HOME

WHY READING AND SINGING WITH YOUR CHILD IS SO IMPORTANT

Daily reading with your child leads to increased academic achievement. Music and songs, specifically rhyming songs, are a fun and easy way to build early literacy and language development. Music skills correlate significantly with both phonological awareness and reading development. Singing helps build vocabulary and speech development. And reading and appreciating music together is a wonderful way to strengthen your relationship.

READ AND SING EVERY DAY!

TIPS FOR USING CANTATA LEARNING BOOKS AND SONGS DURING YOUR DAILY STORY TIME

1. As you sing and read, point out the different words on the page that rhyme. Suggest other words that rhyme.

2. Memorize simple rhymes such as Itsy Bitsy Spider and sing them together. This encourages comprehension skills and early literacy skills.

3. Use the questions in the back of each book to guide your singing and storytelling.

4. Read the included sheet music with your child while you listen to the song. How do the music notes correlate to the words of the song?

5. Sing along on the go and at home. Access music by scanning the QR code on each Cantata book. You can also stream or download the music for free to your computer, smartphone, or mobile device.

Devoting time to daily reading shows that you are available for your child. Together, you are building language, literacy, and listening skills.

Have fun reading and singing!

Brown is made by mixing a **primary color** with a **secondary color**. The primary colors are red, yellow, and blue, and the secondary colors are orange, green, and purple. The colors mixed into brown can make it a **warm color** or a **cool color**. Sometimes brown makes us feel wild or brave. Other times it makes us feel calm and comfortable.

There are many ways to make brown, but where can brown be found? Turn the page to find out! Don't forget to sing along!

Brown, oh brown,
where are you found?

Up and down
and all around.

6

Find brown when you go for a walk.
The dirt, the leaves, and all the rock.

Brown can crawl over the ground.

Brown makes webs, brown jumps around.

Brown, oh brown,
where are you found?

Up and down
and all around.

12

Brown gives you a **thrilling** ride.

Brown will stay right by your side.

Brown, oh brown,
where are you found?

Up and down
and all around.

16

Brown tastes salty. Brown tastes sweet.
Brown can get you tapping your feet.

Brown is a song. Brown is a book.

Brown is everywhere you look!

SONG LYRICS
Brown

Brown, oh brown,
where are you found?
Up and down
and all around.

Find brown when you go for a walk.
The dirt, the leaves, and all the rock.

Brown can crawl over the ground.
Brown makes webs, brown jumps around.

Brown, oh brown,
where are you found?
Up and down
and all around.

Brown gives you a thrilling ride.
Brown will stay right by your side.

Brown, oh brown,
where are you found?
Up and down
and all around.

Brown tastes salty. Brown tastes sweet.
Brown can get you tapping your feet.

Brown is a song. Brown is a book.
Brown is everywhere you look!

Brown

Americana
Erik Koskinen

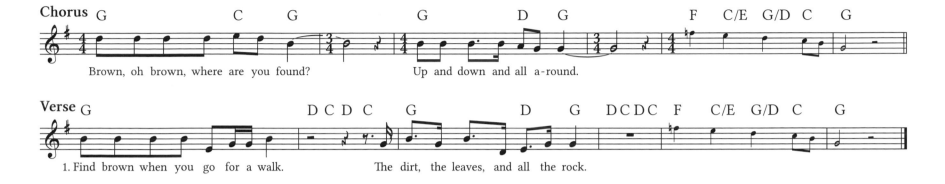

Chorus
Brown, oh brown, where are you found? Up and down and all a-round.

Verse
1. Find brown when you go for a walk. The dirt, the leaves, and all the rock.

Verse 2
Brown can crawl over the ground.
Brown makes webs, brown jumps around.

Chorus

Verse 3
Brown gives you a thrilling ride.
Brown will stay right by your side.

Chorus

Verse 4
Brown tastes salty. Brown tastes sweet.
Brown can get you tapping your feet.

Verse 5
Brown is a song. Brown is a book.
Brown is everywhere you look!

GLOSSARY

cool color—a calm and soothing color that we see in nature, such as blues, purples, and greens

primary colors—colors, such as blue, red, and yellow, mixed to make other colors

secondary colors—colors, such as orange, green, and purple, made by mixing two primary colors

thrilling—very exciting

warm color—a bold and exciting color that we see in nature, such as reds, yellows, and oranges.

GUIDED READING ACTIVITIES

1. Find these brown things in this book: a cricket (a type of bug), a chocolate Labrador dog, an owl, a pretzel. What other brown things can you find?

2. Colors can make us feel different emotions. What feeling or feelings does brown make you feel?

3. Grab your crayons or markers and draw your favorite brown animal. Now draw your favorite brown food.

TO LEARN MORE

Amstutz, Lisa J. *Ants*. North Mankato, MN: Capstone, 2017.

Carole, Bonnie. *Brown and Orange in Fall*. Vero Beach, FL: Rourke Educational Media, 2015.

Nunn, Daniel. *Brown*. Chicago: Heinemann-Raintree, 2012.

Stockland, Patricia M. *Brown*. Minneapolis: Magic Wagon, 2011.